Anyone Can Have a Pet

Story by Nicki Atkinson
Illustrations by Margaret Power

Brad stared down at his desk.
He was hoping that the teacher
might forget to call his name today.

Everyone had been asked to talk
about a pet.
Some children had even brought
their pets to school.

But Brad didn't have a pet.
He lived on the ground floor
of a big apartment building
with his mom.

There was a sign on the wall
that said... **NO PETS**.

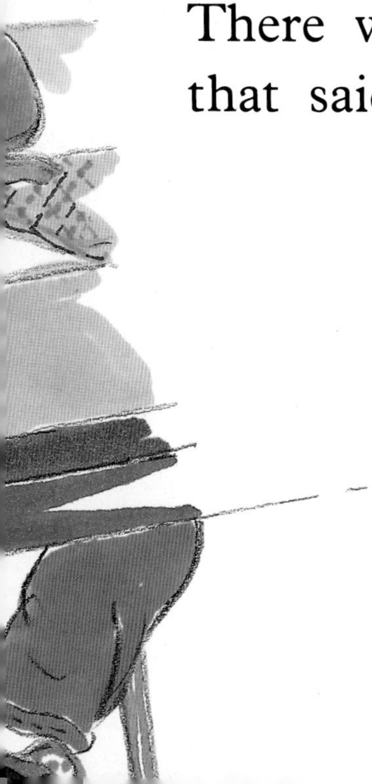

Brad wished his mother
had let him stay at home.

He moved his pencil case away
from his drawing book,
and looked down at his picture
of a bluejay.
He had drawn it at home last night.
Brad loved art,
and he was very proud
of his drawing book.

Brad's friend Josh was standing
in front of the class.
He had his parakeet in a cage.
The parakeet had bright green feathers,
and it was sitting on a little swing.
"Hello, boy!" it squawked to Josh.

Brad wished he had a parakeet.

Kelly had her turn next.
Brad knew she was going to talk about
her cat, Skittles.

Kelly lived across the road
from the school,
and Brad sometimes stopped
to pat Skittles.
He was big and fat,
and he had a grumpy face.
But he always came to see Brad.

Brad wished he had a cat.

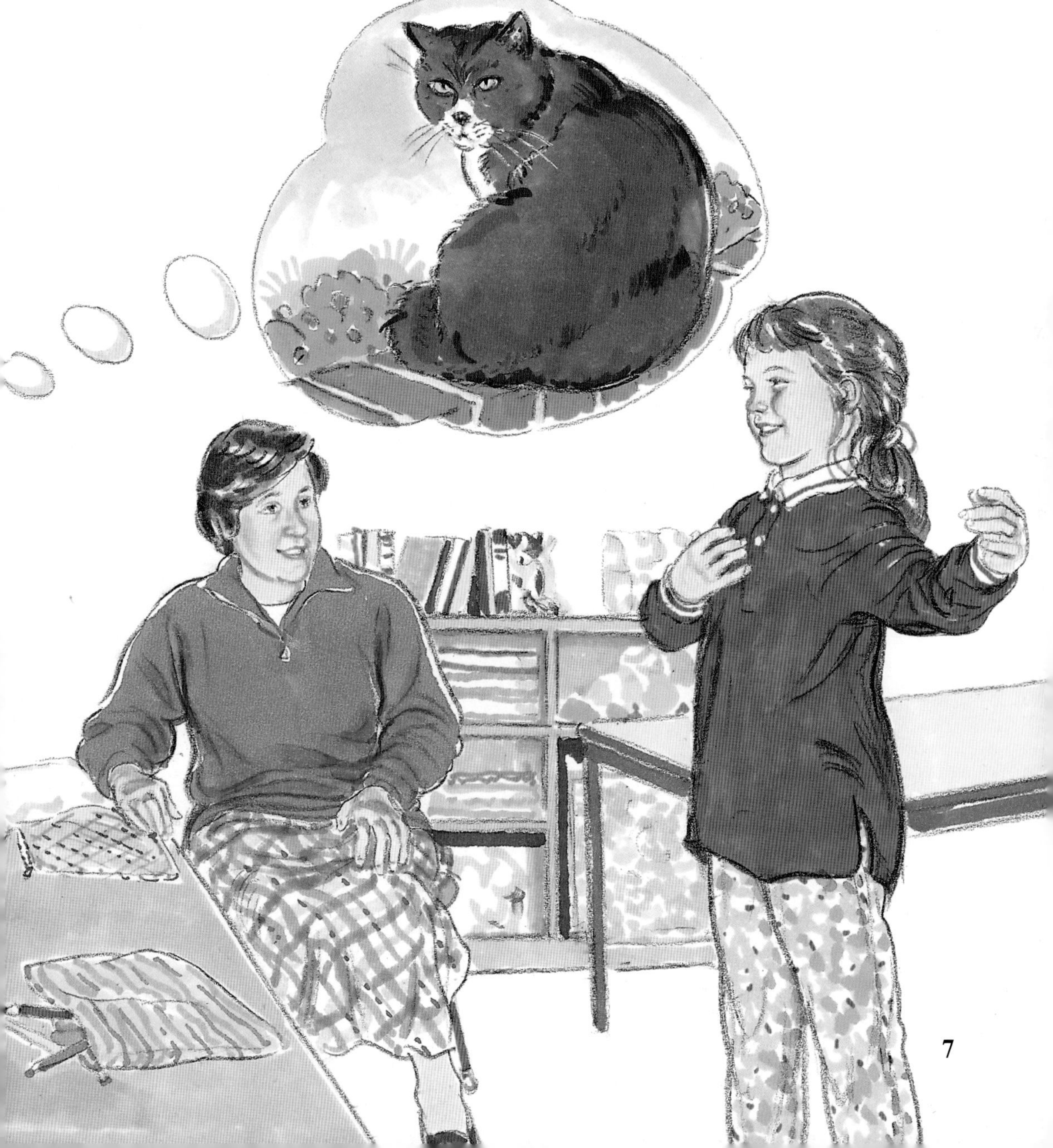

When Kelly sat down,
Benjamin told the class
all about his huge dog named Sandy.
Sometimes, Sandy would pull Benjamin
along on a skateboard.

Brad wished he had a dog.

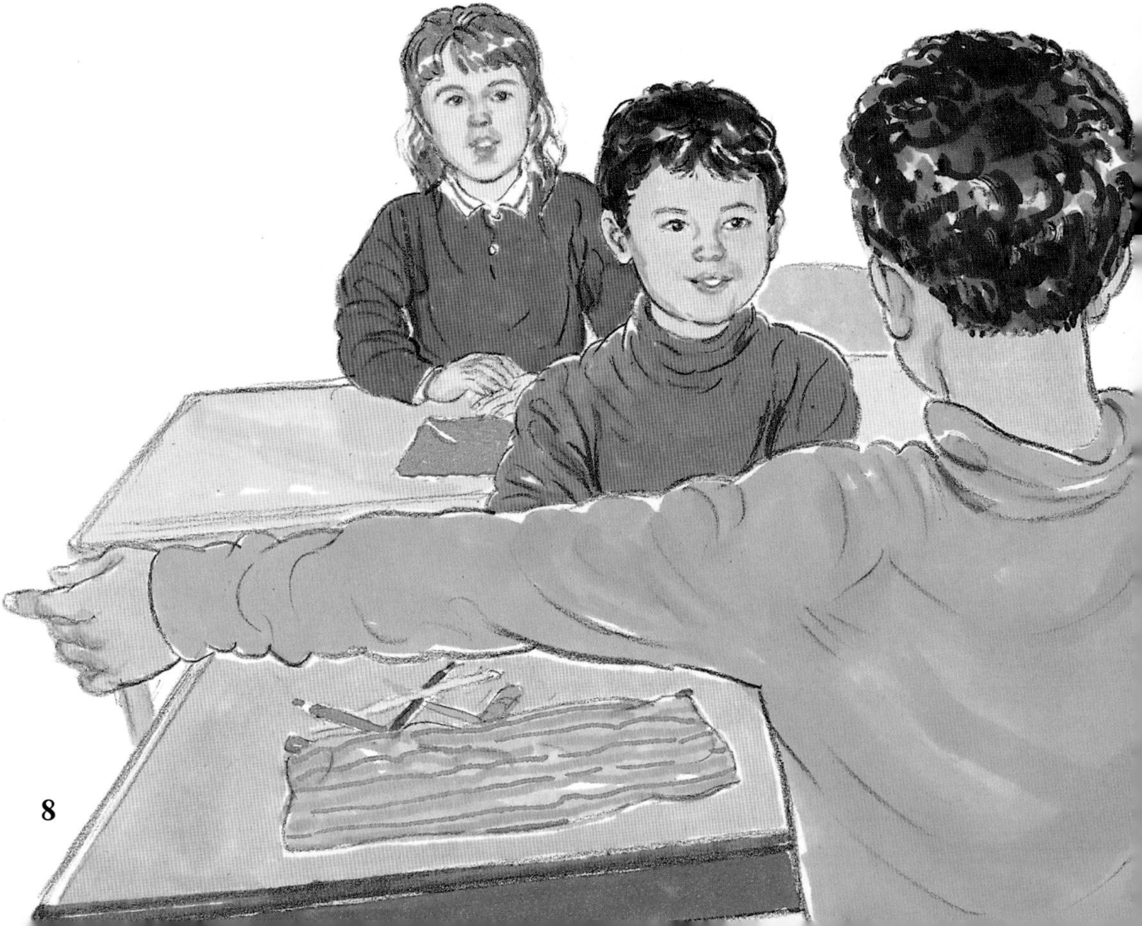

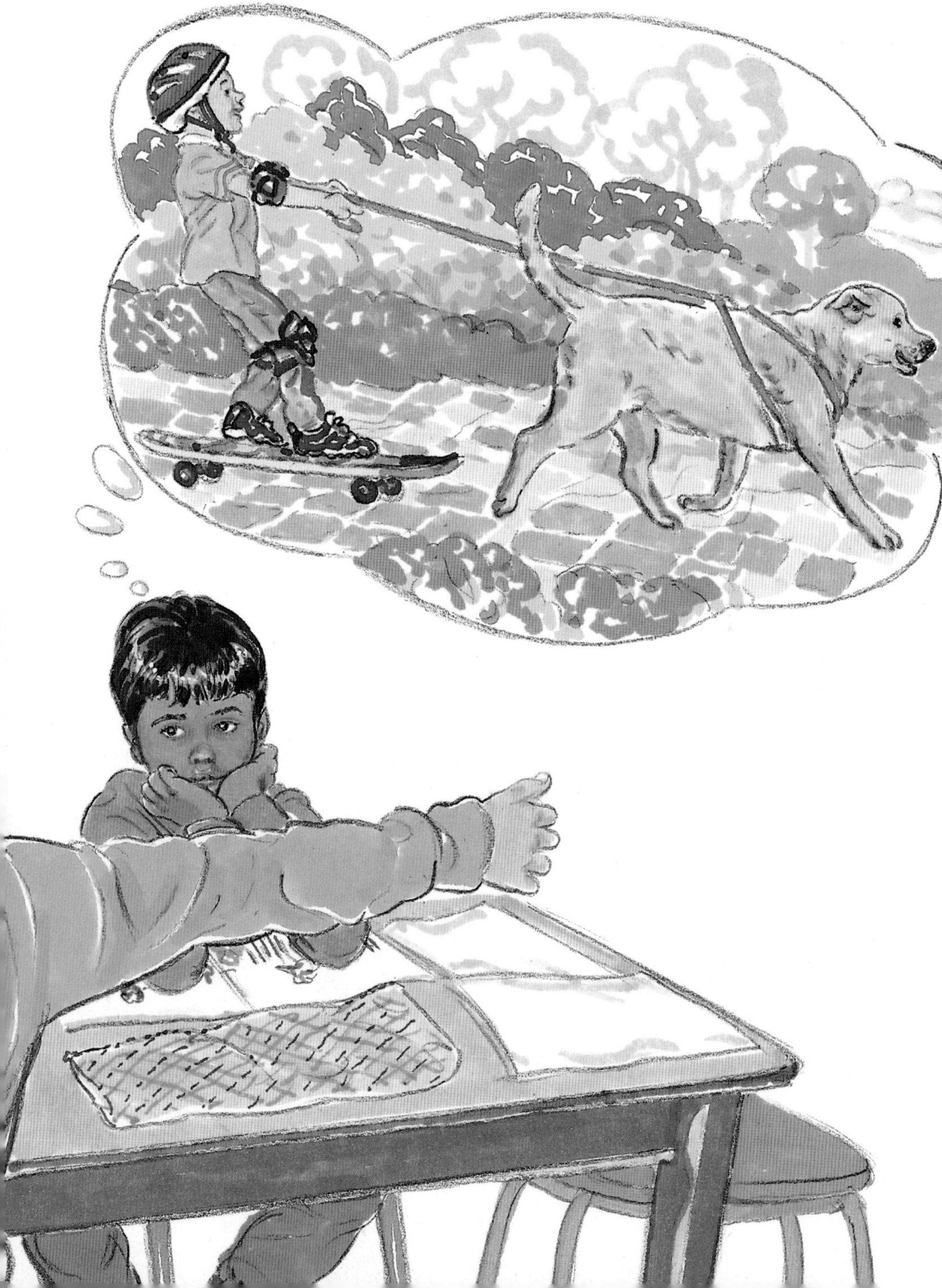

Then the teacher called Brad's name.
Oh no! thought Brad.
He felt like crying.
"I've got nothing to talk about!"
he whispered to Josh.

"Why don't you show everyone
your bluejay?" said Josh.
"You are really good at drawing."

Brad looked at his picture again.
Josh had given him an idea.

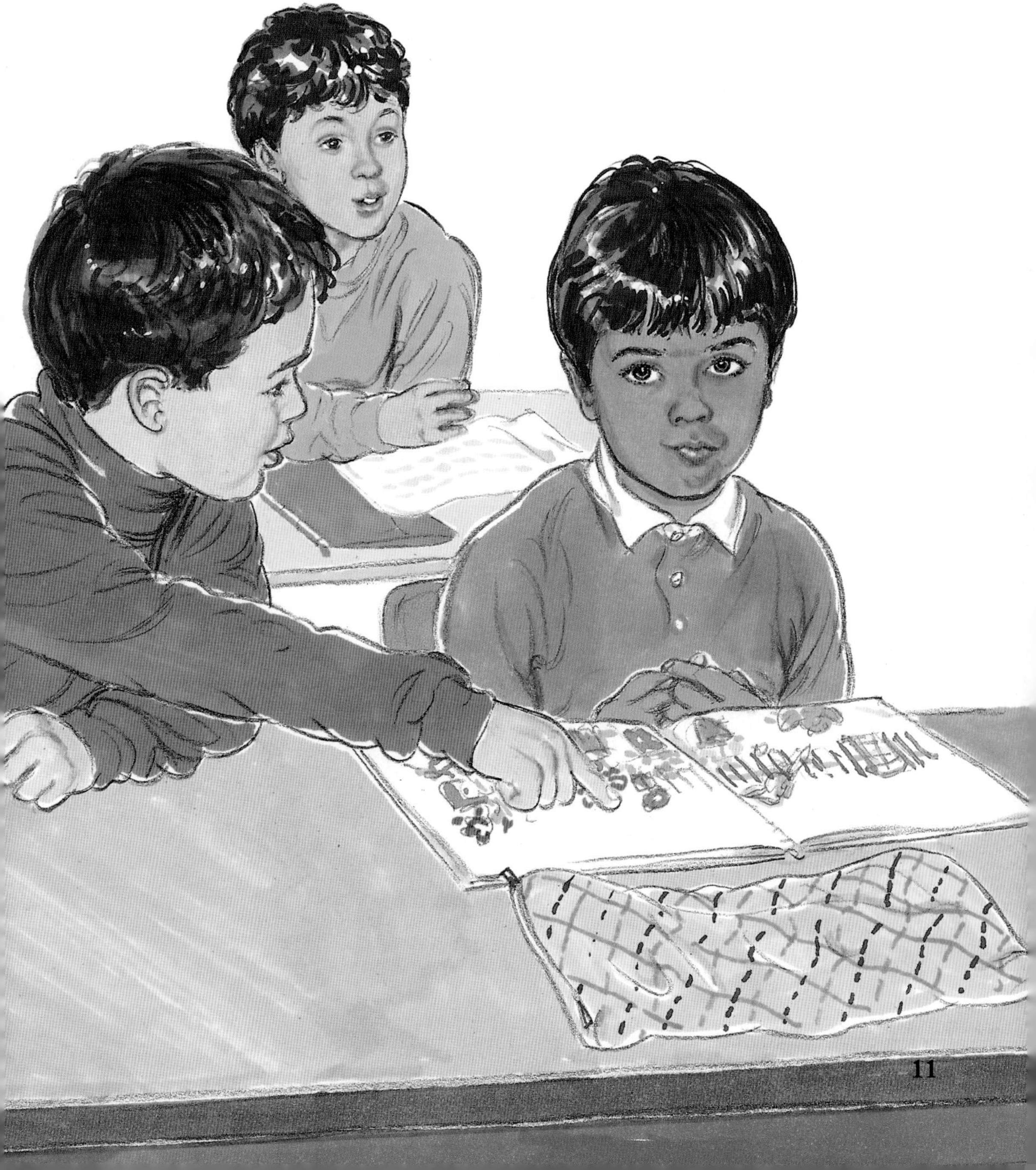

Brad picked up his drawing book,
and walked to the front of the class.
He held up the book and said,
"This bluejay comes to our fence
every afternoon. He flies right down,
and eats seeds from my hand."

All the children leaned forward
in their chairs, looking at the picture.

"Sometimes I tell it a joke," grinned Brad, "and it sounds as if it's laughing at me!"

Brad pointed to a green frog
at the bottom of his picture.
"This frog has made its home
in one of Mom's plants on the patio.
He sits there and watches me
with his big eyes.
Sometimes he calls out to me,
and I talk to him."

Then Brad pointed to some grasshoppers
on the other side of the picture.
"These grasshoppers
come onto our patio, too.
Sometimes Mom chases them away
so they won't eat her plants.
But they always come back.
I like watching them
and talking to them."

Brad smiled at the class.
"I don't really **keep** any pets," he said.
"These animals live around my home.
I feed them, and talk to them,
and play with them.
They come and go
whenever they want to.
They're the sort of pets I have."

And everyone clapped.